ULTIMATE FIRST TIME AUTHOR

BOOK PLANNER

NATASA DENMAN

Cover design: Ultimate World Publishing

Layout and typesetting: Ultimate World Publishing

Editor: Beverley Boorer

ULTIMATE WORLD
—— PUBLISHING ——

Ultimate World Publishing
Diamond Creek,
Victoria Australia 3089
www.writeabook.com.au

AUTHOR NAME:

_____

BOOK RELEASE DATE:

_____

ULTIMATE WORLD
—— PUBLISHING ——

ULTIMATE 48 HOUR
—— A U T H O R ——

So, you want to write your first book? Awesome!!!

Almost ten years ago, I was in the same position you are in now. Unlike you, I had no tools, no education and no strategy as to how I should go about writing my first book. I simply started writing. I finished it in just 80 days and had it self-published three months later. Looking back, I made quite a few mistakes, but don't regret the path I took as it ultimately led me to helping others write their first book and fulfil their dreams of becoming a first-time author.

I now have ten books under my belt and have helped over 350 others intimately through our Ultimate 48 Hour Author retreats and thousands through my workshops, online courses and books. I decided to create this success planner and include the most frequently used resources, templates and guides to help you successfully complete your first book.

Please note that how to use some of these templates is best understood by having read the Ultimate 48 Hour Author book for clearer guidance and details on how to use them with accuracy and success.

Writing a book is like working on a jigsaw puzzle. It has many parts and sections that you need to think about in detail. I have put as much detail here as I would have loved to have when pulling together my own book projects. You can always buy more planners for additional books you may be writing in the future. This is the perfect companion, especially if you love putting pen to paper like I do.

Follow the sections in order and do your best to answer all the questions. Writing your first book is actually not about the book, but about the person you become at the other end of it.

To Your Authoring Success,
Natasa Denman - Ultimate 48 Hour Author (www.writeabook.com.au)

WHERE ARE YOU AT RIGHT NOW?

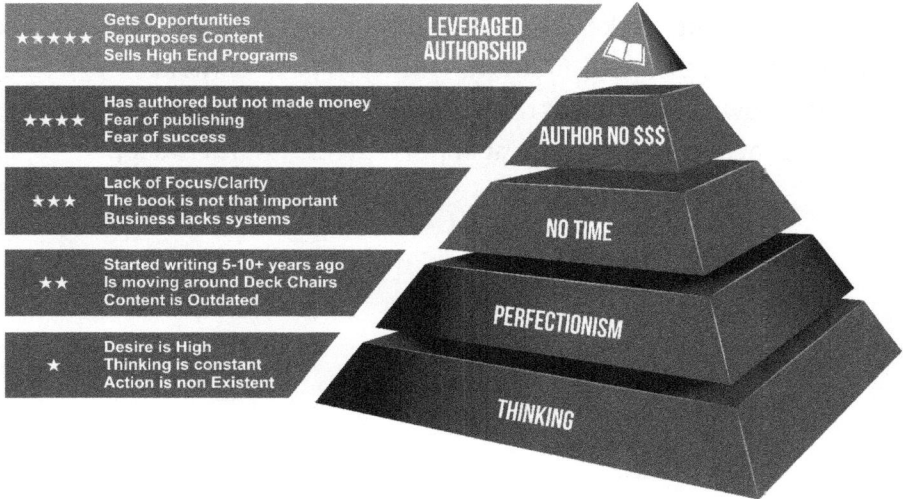

★★★★★	Gets Opportunities Repurposes Content Sells High End Programs	LEVERAGED AUTHORSHIP
★★★★	Has authored but not made money Fear of publishing Fear of success	AUTHOR NO $$$
★★★	Lack of Focus/Clarity The book is not that important Business lacks systems	NO TIME
★★	Started writing 5-10+ years ago Is moving around Deck Chairs Content is Outdated	PERFECTIONISM
★	Desire is High Thinking is constant Action is non Existent	THINKING

Right now, I am sitting at the _____ level of the pyramid.

I've been in this place for _____ years.

I'd like to move to the _____ level of the pyramid.

I'd like to be there by _____.

YOUR BIG 'WHY'

People need reasons before they want answers. Unless you come with a compelling reason why, your success is not guaranteed. This is the page you need to come back to when fear strikes and you feel that you are stuck on your journey to first-time authorship. Document at least 20 reasons below why you want to write your book. Once you have done it, rearrange them so that your most important reason is at the top.

1. _____
2. _____
3. _____
4. _____
5. _____
6. _____
7. _____
8. _____
9. _____
10. _____
11. _____
12. _____
13. _____
14. _____
15. _____
16. _____
17. _____
18. _____
19. _____
20. _____

YOUR KEYS FOR SUCCESS

For you to successfully complete your journey of becoming a first-time author, you need to be aware of the three foundational keys. There are skills you will need to learn and develop, as well as certain obstacles you will need to overcome. Let's look at the three keys:

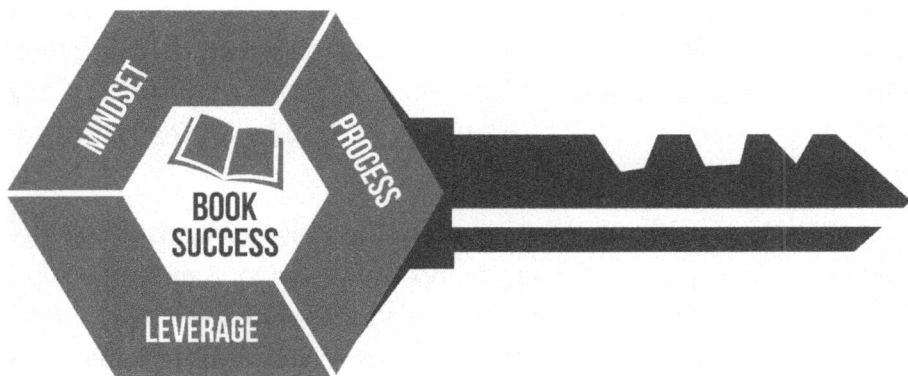

Key 1 is Overcoming Your Mindset – Fear & Self Doubt

Key 2 is Learning the Process – Structure & Publishing

Key 3 is Mastering Leverage – Sales & Marketing

This planner will tackle each of these step by step to help you progress quickly towards the finish line.

The Key I will need most help with is _____

KEY 1 – MINDSET

One of the biggest challenges I have discovered for first-time authors is this key. They think it's lack of understanding the structure, publishing, topic selection, time or money that stands in their way, but almost every single time it is their mindset. Specifically, self-doubt and fear, mostly of success.

In my half-day workshops, I tell my attendees that my biggest challenge that day is to help them get over themselves! I send out my Shut up and Write Your First Book in eBook format to them before the event, as that is the part I need to handle first before we can start talking framework and leverage. If you haven't read that book, I strongly suggest you get your hands on it. My readers say that I touch on a lot of trigger points for them, as if I am inside their heads.

In this section I am going to take you through some statements that I hear all the time from budding authors. I would like you to rank yourself on a scale from 1 to 10 of how much that applies to you (1 being that it doesn't apply and 10 that it does apply very strongly). Then journal your thoughts and beliefs around it and what the new, more empowering beliefs you need to create for yourself to overcome it, are. Strategies on overcoming all these are in Shut up and Write your First Book.

Take some time to really unlock what is going on for you. If you run out of space, use the Notes section at the back of this planner.

1. Who am I to say I am the expert?

Strongly
Disagree 1 2 3 4 5 6 7 8 9 10 Strongly
Agree

_____

_____

_____

_____

_____

_____

2. I am afraid no one will read my book and I will be stuck with a garage full of books.

Strongly
Disagree 1 2 3 4 5 6 7 8 9 10 Strongly
Agree

_____

_____

_____

_____

_____

_____

3. There will be too much pressure if I become successful.

Strongly
Disagree 1 2 3 4 5 6 7 8 9 10 Strongly
Agree

_____

_____

_____

_____

_____

_____

4. I am afraid of criticism and trolls.

Strongly
Disagree   1   2   3   4   5   6   7   8   9   10   Strongly
Agree

_____

_____

_____

_____

_____

_____

5. I just don't have the time

Strongly
Disagree   1   2   3   4   5   6   7   8   9   10   Strongly
Agree

_____

_____

_____

_____

_____

_____

6. It's expensive to self-publish a book

Strongly
Disagree   1   2   3   4   5   6   7   8   9   10   Strongly
Agree

_____

_____

_____

_____

_____

_____

7. I am such a perfectionist.

Strongly
Disagree   1   2   3   4   5   6   7   8   9   10   Strongly
Agree

_____

_____

_____

_____

_____

_____

8. My topic has been written on before. How am I any more special?

Strongly
Disagree   1   2   3   4   5   6   7   8   9   10   Strongly
Agree

_____

_____

_____

_____

_____

_____

9. I have so many ideas. I don't know which one to pick.

Strongly
Disagree   1   2   3   4   5   6   7   8   9   10   Strongly
Agree

_____

_____

_____

_____

_____

_____

10. English not my first language. I have an accent and worry about how good my book will end up being.

Strongly
Disagree   1   2   3   4   5   6   7   8   9   10   Strongly
Agree

_____

_____

_____

_____

_____

_____

11. I just started my business. I don't have many clients. I need to experience and learn more.

Strongly
Disagree   1   2   3   4   5   6   7   8   9   10   Strongly
Agree

_____

_____

_____

_____

_____

_____

12. I am a procrastinator.

Strongly
Disagree   1   2   3   4   5   6   7   8   9   10   Strongly
Agree

_____

_____

_____

_____

_____

_____

13. I don't have much support at home.

Strongly
Disagree   1   2   3   4   5   6   7   8   9   10   Strongly
Agree

_____

_____

_____

_____

_____

14. I am worried about the legal issues that may arise from my content.

Strongly
Disagree   1   2   3   4   5   6   7   8   9   10   Strongly
Agree

_____

_____

_____

_____

_____

15. I am a great starter, but find it difficult to finish.

Strongly
Disagree   1   2   3   4   5   6   7   8   9   10   Strongly
Agree

_____

_____

_____

_____

_____

16. I am worried my book will be no good.

Strongly Disagree   1   2   3   4   5   6   7   8   9   10   Strongly Agree

_____

_____

_____

_____

_____

17. I have been writing for 5-10 years.

Strongly Disagree   1   2   3   4   5   6   7   8   9   10   Strongly Agree

_____

_____

_____

_____

_____

18. You need to be a special kind of person to become an author.

Strongly Disagree   1   2   3   4   5   6   7   8   9   10   Strongly Agree

_____

_____

_____

_____

_____

19. My topic will be hard to sell.

Strongly
Disagree   1 2 3 4 5 6 7 8 9 10   Strongly
Agree

_____

_____

_____

_____

_____

_____

20. I feel that if I commit, the book will take over my life...

Strongly
Disagree   1 2 3 4 5 6 7 8 9 10   Strongly
Agree

_____

_____

_____

_____

_____

_____

Well done on completing your mindset essentials. Watch out for some of these popping back up during your journey. Even when we think we have handled our fear, it can sneak up on us from nowhere if triggered.

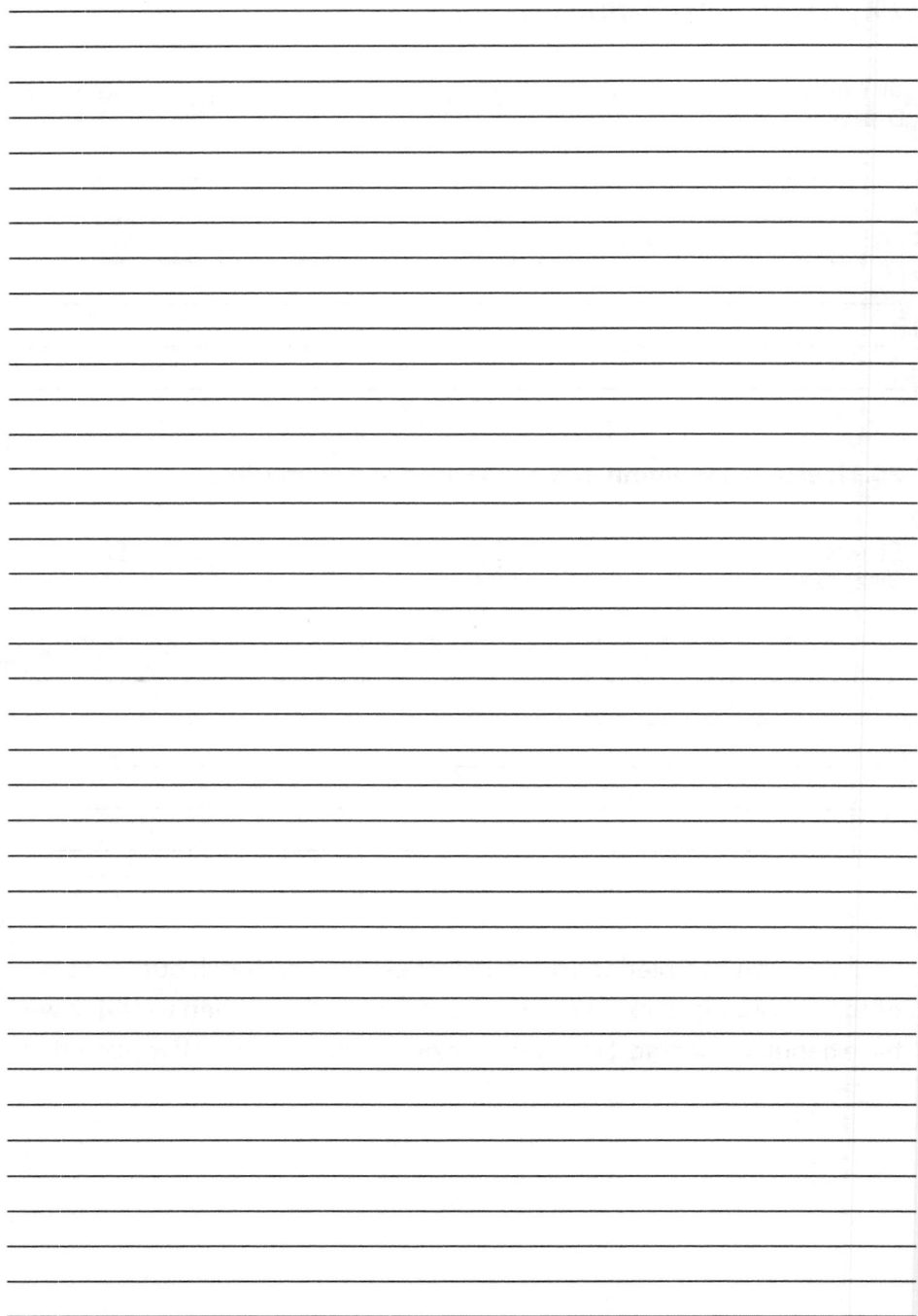

A WORD ON RESISTANCE

Stepping outside of our comfort zone can run havoc in our subconscious mind. I have found many blockages come up in authors' ways just as they are about to take the leap of faith on this journey, or as they move along the path. Watch out for what that could mean for you. People have caught a nasty cold, missed a flight, have had family or work emergencies, or unforeseen events have come up at times just as they are about to have a breakthrough. We often manifest these situations to keep ourselves safe from what we think becoming an author will mean for us. It is our prehistoric critter brain thinking it's a life or death situation and thus producing some interesting roadblocks.

The best way to handle resistance is to acknowledge it with awareness and proceed anyway. It's kind of the universe's test: Are you worthy of your success?

Notes

_____

_____

_____

_____

_____

_____

_____

_____

_____

_____

_____

_____

_____

GOAL SETTING FOR SUCCESS

With your 'Why' and your Mindset Essentials unravelled, it is time to set the scene for your authoring journey and set your goals. Remember, goal setting it is not the goal that you are after, but the feeling you will have when you've achieved it. In the next pages you will find templates on designing your 5-Year Vision, setting your 12-month and 90-day goals.

For your 5-Year Vision, simply put the year 5 years from now. For your 12-month and 90-day goals, insert the appropriate dates from now. Eg. If its 20 March 2020, in 12 month it will be 20 March 2021 and in 90 days 20 June 2020. Insert these dates in the allocated spots.

I recommend setting the 12-month goals first, then the first 90-day goals. When you get close to the end of the first 90 days, set the following 90 days.

We often overestimate what we can achieve in a shorter period of time and underestimate what we can achieve in a longer period of time. There are further goal setting instructions on the upcoming pages.

Notes

_____
_____
_____
_____
_____
_____
_____
_____
_____

My 5 Year Vision

At the end of each line write in about your environment in 5 years time.
What are you doing, what is around you, the things you have etc.

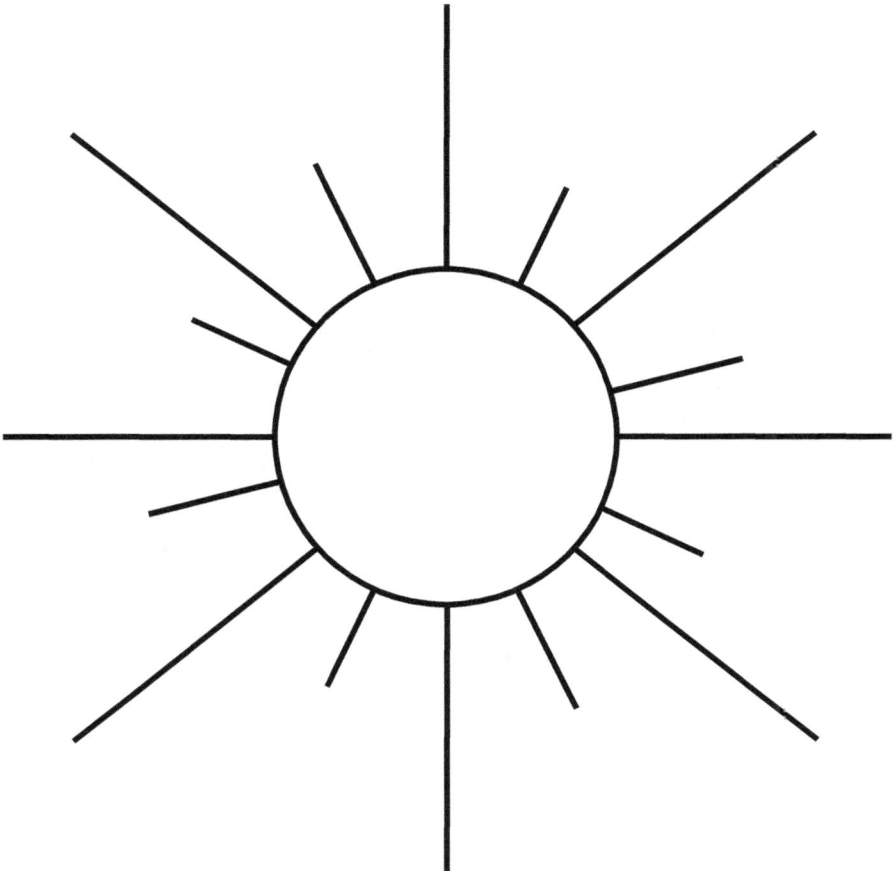

Setting Your Ultimate Goals

Goals are super powerful intentions that if set correctly can really take your life and business to the next level. It is important to make sure you calibrate your journey along the way. Some things you set on 1st of Jan may not be relevant later in the year and others may seem so far out of reach, but never lose faith in things turning around and you absolutely smashing them.

Key things you must remember when setting your goals using the templates provided are:

- Write in the Present tense 'As If' you are in possession of your goal.

- Be Specific, Have Measurements, make it Attainable yet Realistic and finally put a Time Frame on it.

- Engage your modalities of Visual, Auditory and Kinaesthetic. What will you Feel, Hear and See when you have achieved your goal? This is key for the attainment of your goals as we are after the emotion we experience more so than the actual goal.

I always aim at 70-80% success rate with my goals as a minimum. If I get 100% I am really excited and happy, although as I set goals that really stretch me (yet they are still realistic) 70-80% is a fantastic achievement all the more.

Here are three questions to ask yourself if you keep missing the mark:
1. Is your WHY strong enough?
2. Are your goals Realistic?
3. Are you taking Action?

There are three key things that occur when you set goals:
1. Tension in your brain
2. Commitment
3. Ownership

Tension in your brain – you create this with the sheer fact that you are not where you want to be. This tension is good, if not great. It moves you to action. It makes you feel uncomfortable and motivated to get to where you have said you

want to go. Use it to your advantage and you will achieve amazing results going forward.

Commitment – setting pen to paper is super powerful. The sheer fact that you are writing down what you want to achieve engages a couple of your senses. Visually you can see your goal in front of you and kinaesthetically you feel yourself committing it to paper. Also reading your goals out loud and with conviction engages the auditory sense – a great way to add more oomph to the power of goal setting.

Ownership – the end you have in mind is different to everyone else's. You are unique and your standards are just that – your own. So do take responsibility for your results and set what you want, not what others want for you. Goal Setting creates the feeling of being in charge of your destiny. Choose not to drift but decide what will happen and how you will see it to reality.

I encourage you to divide your goals in five key areas:
1. Health/Wellness
2. Personal Development
3. Business/Career
4. Family/Relationships
5. Financial/Materialistic

Goal Setting is all about stretching yourself to experience new levels of success, abundance and growth in all areas of your life. After all, if you are not growing what is happening instead? One of my favourite sayings is:

You are either Green and Growing or Ripe and Rotting

People who have lived the longest lives filled with abundance and happiness are those that have stretched and set new levels of achievement for themselves, even post retirement.

Start setting your intentions regularly, commit to yourself and live a life of purpose.

Enjoy using the Natasa Denman Method of Goal Setting.

ULTIMATE 12 MONTH GOALS

It's the _____ and I...

	Achieved YES / NO SUCCESS PERCENTAGE _____ %
Reward:	
	Achieved YES / NO SUCCESS PERCENTAGE _____ %
Reward:	
	Achieved YES / NO SUCCESS PERCENTAGE _____ %
Reward:	
	Achieved YES / NO SUCCESS PERCENTAGE _____ %
Reward:	
	Achieved YES / NO SUCCESS PERCENTAGE _____ %
Reward:	

ULTIMATE 1st QUARTER GOALS

It's the _____ and I...

	Achieved YES / NO SUCCESS PERCENTAGE _____ %
Reward:	
	Achieved YES / NO SUCCESS PERCENTAGE _____ %
Reward:	
	Achieved YES / NO SUCCESS PERCENTAGE _____ %
Reward:	
	Achieved YES / NO SUCCESS PERCENTAGE _____ %
Reward:	
	Achieved YES / NO SUCCESS PERCENTAGE _____ %
Reward:	

ULTIMATE 2nd QUARTER GOALS

It's the _____ and I...

	Achieved YES / NO SUCCESS PERCENTAGE _____ %
Reward:	
	Achieved YES / NO SUCCESS PERCENTAGE _____ %
Reward:	
	Achieved YES / NO SUCCESS PERCENTAGE _____ %
Reward:	
	Achieved YES / NO SUCCESS PERCENTAGE _____ %
Reward:	
	Achieved YES / NO SUCCESS PERCENTAGE _____ %
Reward:	

ULTIMATE 3rd QUARTER GOALS

It's the _____ and I...

	Achieved YES / NO SUCCESS PERCENTAGE _____ %
Reward:	
	Achieved YES / NO SUCCESS PERCENTAGE _____ %
Reward:	
	Achieved YES / NO SUCCESS PERCENTAGE _____ %
Reward:	
	Achieved YES / NO SUCCESS PERCENTAGE _____ %
Reward:	
	Achieved YES / NO SUCCESS PERCENTAGE _____ %
Reward:	

ULTIMATE 4th QUARTER GOALS

It's the _____ and I...

	Achieved YES / NO SUCCESS PERCENTAGE _____ %
Reward:	
	Achieved YES / NO SUCCESS PERCENTAGE _____ %
Reward:	
	Achieved YES / NO SUCCESS PERCENTAGE _____ %
Reward:	
	Achieved YES / NO SUCCESS PERCENTAGE _____ %
Reward:	
	Achieved YES / NO SUCCESS PERCENTAGE _____ %
Reward:	

Ultimate 48 Hour Author Deadlines:

I will be holding my book on _____.

My 2 Hour Prep session is on _____ at _____.

I will work on my pre-retreat checklist on:

	Date	Time	Put in Planner
1.			
2.			
3.			
4.			
5.			
6.			
7.			
8.			
9.			
10.			
11.			
12.			

My Ultimate 48 Hour Author Retreat is on _____

My flights are coming in on _____

My flights going out are _____

I will submit my recordings for transcription by _____

I will work on the clean up of my chapters on:

	Date	Time	Put in Planner
1.	_____	_____	_____
2.	_____	_____	_____
3.	_____	_____	_____
4.	_____	_____	_____
5.	_____	_____	_____
6.	_____	_____	_____
7.	_____	_____	_____
8.	_____	_____	_____
9.	_____	_____	_____
10.	_____	_____	_____
11.	_____	_____	_____
12.	_____	_____	_____

I will pull together my manuscript on:

	Date	Time	Put in Planner
1.	_____	_____	_____
2.	_____	_____	_____
3.	_____	_____	_____

I will submit my manuscript on _____

My book launch is on _____

I will start planning my launch on _____

I will go to Print on _____

CONGRATULATIONS ON BECOMING AN AUTHOR!

KEY 2 - PROCESS

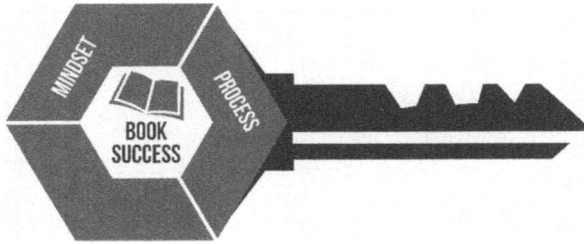

YOUR BOOK PATHWAY

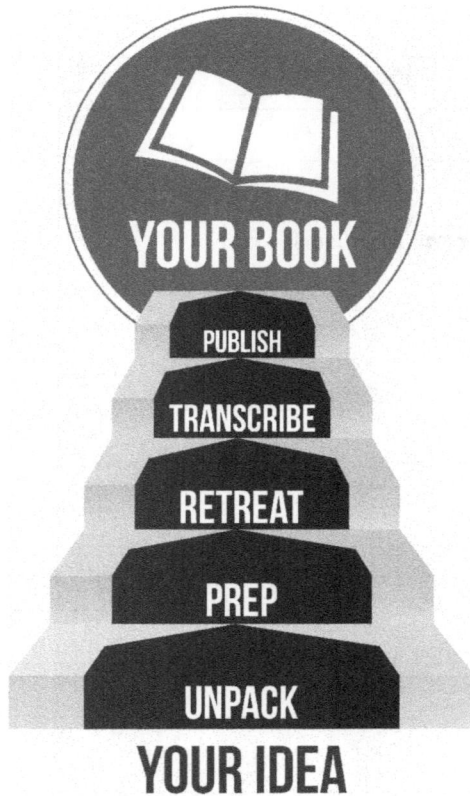

YOUR BOOK

PUBLISH

TRANSCRIBE

RETREAT

PREP

UNPACK

YOUR IDEA

IDEAL CLIENT DESCRIPTION
A.K.A. NO DICKHEADS POLICY

Very early on in my business, I started writing about whom I wanted to attract into my life when it came to clients. My husband and I then started making it an annual tradition that each January during our family road trip we would review the previous year's 'No dickheads policy' and write out new one for the year ahead.

This way we were very clear about who we would like to attract, who we would work with and who we would disqualify as they were not a match for our personalities and business. This stuff is powerful and so accurate. It always amazes me how much clarity and focus it gives us on who is good for us.

I challenge you to create your own 'No dickheads policy' in the space below. To give you a starting point, think about your ideal client's personality, communication style, decision making, financial position and behaviour, their awareness level, ability to remain solution focussed, ability to remain coachable and resourceful, their referral profile and your relationship with them.

Notes

_____
_____
_____
_____
_____
_____
_____

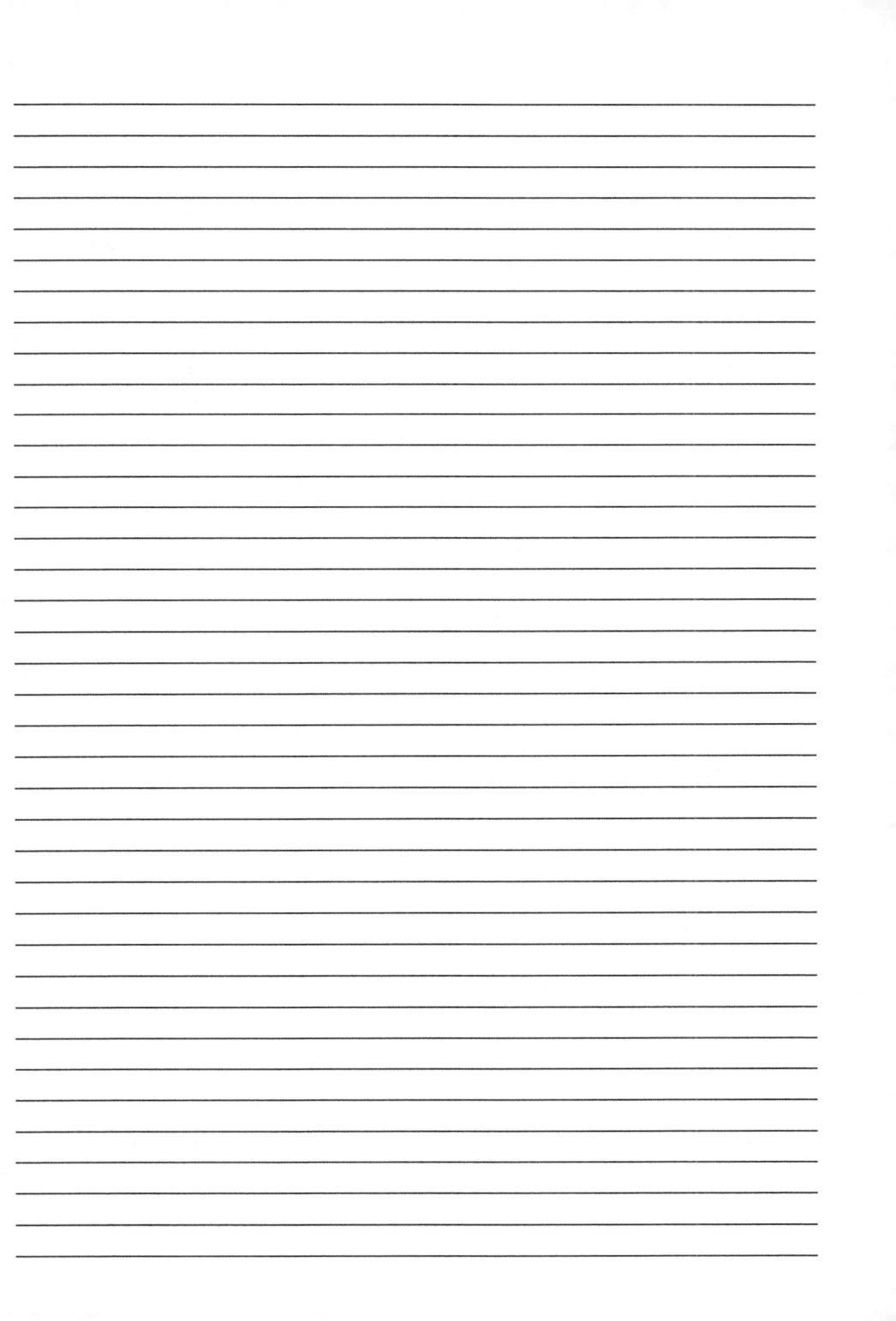

SEXY HYPNOTIC WORDS

We are about to unpack your book, but before we do that you need to learn the power of sexy hypnotic words and phrases. The internet would have thousands if you simple Google 'hypnotic words'. Here I will give you a list I share with my clients to give them a jump start.

You will be using these to name your book, in your tagline, chapter names, offers, sales copyrighting and the back of your book (the blurb).

A Gallery of	A Sampler of	Absolutely	Accomplish
Achieve	Affordable	Alert	Allure
Alluring	Alternative	Amazing	Announcing
Approved	Attain	Attractive	Authentic
Avoiding	Bargain	Beautiful	Beauty
Benefit from	Better	Big	Blast
Blockbuster	Bonanza	Bonus	Boom
Boost	Breakthrough	Burst	Buyer's Guide
Challenge	Challenging	Colourful	Colossal
Compare	Competitive	Complete	Comprehensive
Compromise	Concept	Confidential	Crammed

Crucial	Customized	Daring	Dazzling
Delicious	Delivered	Destiny	Direct
Discount	Discover	Distinguished	Dynamics
Dynamite	Earn	Easily	Easy
Effective	Electrifying	Emerging	Endorsed
Endurance	Energising	Energy	Enjoy
Enormous	Enterprising	Envision	Excellent
Excitement	Exciting	Exclusive	Exercising
Expert	Explode	Explosive	Facts
Famous	Fascinating	Find	Floodgates
Flourish	Focus	Foothold	Forecast
Formula	Fortune	Free	Fuelling
Full	Fun	Fundamentals	Garner
Genuine	Get	Gift	Gigantic
Grasp	Greatest	Growth	Guaranteed
Harvest	Health	Helpful	High Tech
High Yield	Highest	Hot	How

Huge	Hurry	Imagination	Imagine
Immediately	Important	Improved	Increase
Incredible	Informative	Innovative	Insatiable
Instantly	Instructive	Interesting	Introducing
Investigative	Just In Time	Largest	Last Minute
Late-Breaking	Latest	Lavishly	Liberated
Lifetime	Limited	Limited Time Offer	Lively
Look	Lowest	Luxury	Magic
Mainstream	Mammoth	Masterpiece	Merit
Mind-Blowing	Miracle	Money	Money-Back
Monumental	Mouth-Watering	New	Next Frontier
Noted	Novel	Now	Obsession
Obtain	Odd	Only	Opportunities
Outstanding	Own	Personalized	Perspective
Philosophy	Pioneering	Plus	Popular
Portfolio	Potent	Potential	Power
Powerful	Practical	Professional	Profit From

Profitable	Profits	Promising	Protect
Proven	Provocative	Quality	Quick
Quickly	Rare	Reap	Reduced
Refundable	Reliable	Remarkable	Results
Revealing	Reveals	Revolutionary	Rewards
Safely	Sale	Save	Savvy
Scarce	Scorecard	Secrets	Secure
Security	Seductive	Selected	Sensational
Shocking	Simplified	Simplistic	Sizable
Sizzling	Skill	Soar	Solution
Special	Specialised	Spotlight	Starter Kit
Startling	Stop	Strange	Strong
Stunning	Sturdy	Successful	Suddenly
Superior	Sure-Fire	Surging	Surprise
Surprising	Survival	Technology	Terrific
Test Drive	Tested	Thrilling	Time Sensitive
Timely	Tremendous	Trusted	Truth

Ultimate	Unconditional	Uncover	Under Priced
Unique	Unleash	Unlimited	Unlock
Unparalleled	Unsurpassed	Unusual	Up Scale
Urgent	Useful	Valuable	Vital
Vivid	Want	Wanted	Warning
Wealth	Willpower	Win	Winning
Wonderful	Yes	You	You're

UNPACKING YOUR BOOK

On the following pages you will find our book unpack template. I have given you a few copies as you may find that you want to attempt it a few times and rearrange the order of your chapters once you are happy with one. It can take a few goes to get it the way you want it. Also, when you are writing each of your chapters, you may want to re-adjust the name of that chapter to fit the content even better.

It is very important to fill out the page first before the chapter topics, as this will give you clues and ideas about what to put in the book. At this time you are only thinking at high level, not detail. It is best to start with the big picture/chunks and when work backwards chunking it down.

Refer to Chapter 2 in the Ultimate 48 Hour Author book (page 17) for an in depth explanation of how to use this template properly and how to sexy up your chapter names on the right hand side.

ULTIMATE BOOK UNPACK

Purpose (the things I would like to see the book do for me and my business)

_____

_____

_____

_____

_____

_____

Target Market (include their pain points, wants and needs):

_____

_____

_____

_____

_____

_____

Problem being solved:

_____

_____

_____

_____

_____

Please note: If your book is a personal story, the answers to these questions may not be relevant, although you will still have an ideal target readership you'll need to keep in mind when writing the book.

Ch	Broad Topic (Needs)	Sexy Name (Wants)	Order
1			
2			
3			
4			
5			
6			
7			
8			
9			
10			
11			
12			

Book Title: _____

Tagline: _____

ULTIMATE BOOK UNPACK

Purpose (the things I would like to see the book do for me and my business)

_____
_____
_____
_____
_____
_____

Target Market (include their pain points, wants and needs):

_____
_____
_____
_____
_____
_____

Problem being solved:

_____
_____
_____
_____
_____
_____

Please note: If your book is a personal story, the answers to these questions may not be relevant, although you will still have an ideal target readership you'll need to keep in mind when writing the book.

Ch	Broad Topic (Needs)	Sexy Name (Wants)	Order
1			
2			
3			
4			
5			
6			
7			
8			
9			
10			
11			
12			

Book Title: _____

Tagline: _____

ULTIMATE BOOK UNPACK

Purpose (the things I would like to see the book do for me and my business)

_____

_____

_____

_____

_____

_____

Target Market (include their pain points, wants and needs):

_____

_____

_____

_____

_____

Problem being solved:

_____

_____

_____

_____

_____

Please note: If your book is a personal story, the answers to these questions may not be relevant, although you will still have an ideal target readership you'll need to keep in mind when writing the book.

Ch	Broad Topic (Needs)	Sexy Name (Wants)	Order
1			
2			
3			
4			
5			
6			
7			
8			
9			
10			
11			
12			

Book Title: _____

Tagline: _____

ULTIMATE BOOK UNPACK

Purpose (the things I would like to see the book do for me and my business)

_____

_____

_____

_____

_____

_____

Target Market (include their pain points, wants and needs):

_____

_____

_____

_____

_____

_____

Problem being solved:

_____

_____

_____

_____

_____

_____

Please note: If your book is a personal story, the answers to these questions may not be relevant, although you will still have an ideal target readership you'll need to keep in mind when writing the book.

Ch	Broad Topic (Needs)	Sexy Name (Wants)	Order
1			
2			
3			
4			
5			
6			
7			
8			
9			
10			
11			
12			

Book Title: _____

Tagline: _____

UNPACKING YOUR CHAPTERS

Depending on the type of book you are writing, you will use one of these two chapter unpack templates. It's a lot simpler for personal stories than for 'How to' books. Please refer to page 36 and 37 for a deeper understanding of how to use this template. Chapter 3 in the book, covers exactly how to use both templates in great detail.

I will share just one personal story template here and include 15 'How to' style templates so you can take the time to unpack in detail your 12 chapters. You can quite easily use the Notes pages or blank paper to unpack a personal story style book.

Unpacking your chapters will be the most time-consuming part of your book preparation. I suggest tackling it early. The more you use the templates, the faster you will get. Initially, it may take you 60-90 minutes to complete one, but as you become more familiar with them, you will be able to get them down to 30 minutes. I can now unpack my content for chapters in just 7 minutes.

This template is said to be one of the most valuable resources of the whole Ultimate 48 Hour Author programme. It will also help you in creating keynotes, other presentations and write book after book once you master it. It is awkward at the beginning, but it does become easier.

The order in which I have placed things in this planner is the order I recommend you complete the work in. Trust the process and someone who has written ten books and helped over 350 others do it.

The 'How to' template in this planner is split across 2 pages as it normally just sits on one A4 page. Complete the sections in the order presented.

Personal Story Chapter Unpack Template (17-20min of speaking) 3000-3300 words

Chapter Name: _____

Set the Scene Notes:

_____

_____

_____

5 Key Stories/Defining Moments:

1. _____

Learning:_____

_____

2. _____

Learning:_____

_____

3. _____

Learning:_____

_____

4. _____

Learning:_____

_____

5. _____

Learning:_____

_____

Summary Points:

_____

_____

_____

'How to' Style Book – Chapter Unpack Template

Chapter Name: _____

Opening Sentence:

_____

_____

_____

1. WHY: (Start Here) **(25% 5-7min)**

1. _____

2. _____

3. _____

4. _____

5. _____

Fact/Statistic/Shocking truth (1):

_____

_____

Quotes (2): Google relevant quotesfor this chapter.

Contrast/Pain (1):

_____

_____

2. WHAT: **(5% 1min)** Define each term

_____

_____

_____

_____

_____

_____

_____

_____

3. HOW: (60% 10-12mins)

3 different ways to teach the WHAT using Stories to illustrate it...

1._____

_____

2._____

_____

3._____

_____

4. WHAT IF: (10% 3-5min)

Objections and responses (1-3):

O1:_____

R1: _____

O2:_____

R2: _____

O3:_____

R3: _____

3 actions the reader should take as a result of reading this chapter:

1._____

2._____

3._____

Additional information/resources:

_____

_____

_____

_____

_____

_____

_____

'How to' Style Book – Chapter Unpack Template

Chapter Name: _____

Opening Sentence:

_____

_____

_____

1. WHY: (Start Here) **(25% 5-7min)**

1. _____

2. _____

3. _____

4. _____

5. _____

Fact/Statistic/Shocking truth (1):

_____

_____

Quotes (2): Google relevant quotesfor this chapter.

Contrast/Pain (1):

_____

_____

2. WHAT: **(5% 1min)** Define each term

_____

_____

_____

_____

_____

_____

_____

_____

3. HOW: (60% 10-12mins)

3 different ways to teach the WHAT using Stories to illustrate it...

1._____

_____

2._____

_____

3._____

_____

4. WHAT IF: (10% 3-5min)

Objections and responses (1-3):

O1:_____

R1: _____

O2:_____

R2: _____

O3:_____

R3: _____

3 actions the reader should take as a result of reading this chapter:

1._____

2._____

3._____

Additional information/resources:

_____

_____

_____

_____

_____

_____

_____

'How to' Style Book – Chapter Unpack Template

Chapter Name: _____

Opening Sentence:

_____

_____

_____

1. WHY: (Start Here) **(25% 5-7min)**

1. _____

2. _____

3. _____

4. _____

5. _____

Fact/Statistic/Shocking truth (1):

_____

_____

Quotes (2): Google relevant quotesfor this chapter.

Contrast/Pain (1):

_____

_____

2. WHAT: **(5% 1min)** Define each term

_____

_____

_____

_____

_____

_____

_____

3. HOW: (60% 10-12mins)

3 different ways to teach the WHAT using Stories to illustrate it...

1._____

_____

2._____

_____

3._____

_____

4. WHAT IF: (10% 3-5min)

Objections and responses (1-3):

O1:_____

R1:_____

O2:_____

R2:_____

O3:_____

R3:_____

3 actions the reader should take as a result of reading this chapter:

1._____

2._____

3._____

Additional information/resources:

_____

_____

_____

_____

_____

_____

_____

'How to' Style Book – Chapter Unpack Template

Chapter Name: _____

Opening Sentence:

_____

_____

_____

1. WHY: (Start Here) **(25% 5-7min)**

1. _____

2. _____

3. _____

4. _____

5. _____

Fact/Statistic/Shocking truth (1):

_____

_____

Quotes (2): Google relevant quotesfor this chapter.

Contrast/Pain (1):

_____

_____

2. WHAT: **(5% 1min)** Define each term

_____

_____

_____

_____

_____

_____

_____

3. HOW: (60% 10-12mins)

3 different ways to teach the WHAT using Stories to illustrate it...

1._____

_____

2._____

_____

3._____

_____

4. WHAT IF: (10% 3-5min)

Objections and responses (1-3):

O1:_____

R1: _____

O2:_____

R2: _____

O3:_____

R3: _____

3 actions the reader should take as a result of reading this chapter:

1._____

2._____

3._____

Additional information/resources:

_____

_____

_____

_____

_____

_____

_____

'How to' Style Book – Chapter Unpack Template

Chapter Name: _____

Opening Sentence:

_____

_____

_____

1. WHY: (Start Here) **(25% 5-7min)**

1. _____

2. _____

3. _____

4. _____

5. _____

Fact/Statistic/Shocking truth (1):

_____

_____

Quotes (2): Google relevant quotesfor this chapter.

Contrast/Pain (1):

_____

_____

2. WHAT: **(5% 1min)** Define each term

_____

_____

_____

_____

_____

_____

_____

_____

3. HOW: (60% 10-12mins)

3 different ways to teach the WHAT using Stories to illustrate it...

1._____

_____

2._____

_____

3._____

_____

4. WHAT IF: (10% 3-5min)

Objections and responses (1-3):

O1:_____

R1: _____

O2:_____

R2: _____

O3:_____

R3: _____

3 actions the reader should take as a result of reading this chapter:

1._____

2._____

3._____

Additional information/resources:

_____

_____

_____

_____

_____

_____

_____

'How to' Style Book – Chapter Unpack Template

Chapter Name: _____

Opening Sentence:

_____

_____

_____

1. WHY: (Start Here) **(25% 5-7min)**

1. _____

2. _____

3. _____

4. _____

5. _____

Fact/Statistic/Shocking truth (1):

_____

_____

Quotes (2): Google relevant quotesfor this chapter.

Contrast/Pain (1):

_____

_____

2. WHAT: **(5% 1min)** Define each term

_____

_____

_____

_____

_____

_____

_____

3. HOW: (60% 10-12mins)

3 different ways to teach the WHAT using Stories to illustrate it...

1._____

_____

2._____

_____

3._____

_____

4. WHAT IF: (10% 3-5min)

Objections and responses (1-3):

O1:_____

R1: _____

O2:_____

R2: _____

O3:_____

R3: _____

3 actions the reader should take as a result of reading this chapter:

1._____

2._____

3._____

Additional information/resources:

_____

_____

_____

_____

_____

_____

_____

'How to' Style Book – Chapter Unpack Template

Chapter Name: _____

Opening Sentence:

_____

_____

_____

1. WHY: (Start Here) **(25% 5-7min)**

1. _____

2. _____

3. _____

4. _____

5. _____

Fact/Statistic/Shocking truth (1):

_____

_____

Quotes (2): Google relevant quotesfor this chapter.

Contrast/Pain (1):

_____

_____

2. WHAT: **(5% 1min)** Define each term

_____

_____

_____

_____

_____

_____

_____

_____

3. HOW: (60% 10-12mins)

3 different ways to teach the WHAT using Stories to illustrate it...

1._____

_____

2._____

_____

3._____

_____

4. WHAT IF: (10% 3-5min)

Objections and responses (1-3):

O1: _____

R1: _____

O2: _____

R2: _____

O3: _____

R3: _____

3 actions the reader should take as a result of reading this chapter:

1._____

2._____

3._____

Additional information/resources:

_____

_____

_____

_____

_____

_____

_____

'How to' Style Book – Chapter Unpack Template

Chapter Name: _____

Opening Sentence:

_____

_____

_____

1. WHY: (Start Here) **(25% 5-7min)**

1. _____

2. _____

3. _____

4. _____

5. _____

Fact/Statistic/Shocking truth (1):

_____

_____

Quotes (2): Google relevant quotesfor this chapter.

Contrast/Pain (1):

_____

_____

2. WHAT: **(5% 1min)** Define each term

_____

_____

_____

_____

_____

_____

_____

3. HOW: (60% 10-12mins)

3 different ways to teach the WHAT using Stories to illustrate it...

1._____

_____

2._____

_____

3._____

_____

4. WHAT IF: (10% 3-5min)

Objections and responses (1-3):

O1:_____

R1: _____

O2:_____

R2: _____

O3:_____

R3: _____

3 actions the reader should take as a result of reading this chapter:

1._____

2._____

3._____

Additional information/resources:

_____

_____

_____

_____

_____

_____

_____

'How to' Style Book – Chapter Unpack Template

Chapter Name: _____

Opening Sentence:

_____

_____

_____

1. WHY: (Start Here) **(25% 5-7min)**

1. _____

2. _____

3. _____

4. _____

5. _____

Fact/Statistic/Shocking truth (1):

_____

_____

Quotes (2): Google relevant quotesfor this chapter.

Contrast/Pain (1):

_____

_____

2. WHAT: **(5% 1min)** Define each term

_____

_____

_____

_____

_____

_____

_____

3. HOW: (60% 10-12mins)

3 different ways to teach the WHAT using Stories to illustrate it...

1._____

_____

2._____

_____

3._____

_____

4. WHAT IF: (10% 3-5min)

Objections and responses (1-3):

O1:_____

R1: _____

O2: _____

R2: _____

O3: _____

R3: _____

3 actions the reader should take as a result of reading this chapter:

1._____

2._____

3._____

Additional information/resources:

_____

_____

_____

_____

_____

_____

_____

'How to' Style Book – Chapter Unpack Template

Chapter Name: _____

Opening Sentence:

_____

_____

_____

1. WHY: (Start Here) **(25% 5-7min)**

1. _____

2. _____

3. _____

4. _____

5. _____

Fact/Statistic/Shocking truth (1):

_____

_____

Quotes (2): Google relevant quotesfor this chapter.

Contrast/Pain (1):

_____

_____

2. WHAT: **(5% 1min)** Define each term

_____

_____

_____

_____

_____

_____

_____

3. HOW: (60% 10-12mins)

3 different ways to teach the WHAT using Stories to illustrate it…

1._____

_____

2._____

_____

3._____

_____

4. WHAT IF: (10% 3-5min)

Objections and responses (1-3):

O1: _____

R1: _____

O2: _____

R2: _____

O3: _____

R3: _____

3 actions the reader should take as a result of reading this chapter:

1._____

2._____

3._____

Additional information/resources:

_____

_____

_____

_____

_____

_____

_____

'How to' Style Book – Chapter Unpack Template

Chapter Name: _____

Opening Sentence:

_____

_____

_____

1. WHY: (Start Here) **(25% 5-7min)**

1. _____

2. _____

3. _____

4. _____

5. _____

Fact/Statistic/Shocking truth (1):

_____

_____

Quotes (2): Google relevant quotesfor this chapter.

Contrast/Pain (1):

_____

_____

2. WHAT: **(5% 1min)** Define each term

_____

_____

_____

_____

_____

_____

_____

3. HOW: (60% 10-12mins)

3 different ways to teach the WHAT using Stories to illustrate it...

1._____

_____

2._____

_____

3._____

_____

4. WHAT IF: (10% 3-5min)

Objections and responses (1-3):

O1:_____

R1: _____

O2:_____

R2: _____

O3:_____

R3: _____

3 actions the reader should take as a result of reading this chapter:

1._____

2._____

3._____

Additional information/resources:

_____

_____

_____

_____

_____

_____

_____

'How to' Style Book – Chapter Unpack Template

Chapter Name: _____

Opening Sentence:

_____

_____

_____

1. WHY: (Start Here) **(25% 5-7min)**

1. _____

2. _____

3. _____

4. _____

5. _____

Fact/Statistic/Shocking truth (1):

_____

_____

Quotes (2): Google relevant quotesfor this chapter.

Contrast/Pain (1):

_____

_____

2. WHAT: **(5% 1min)** Define each term

_____

_____

_____

_____

_____

_____

_____

_____

3. HOW: (60% 10-12mins)

3 different ways to teach the WHAT using Stories to illustrate it...

1._____

_____

2._____

_____

3._____

_____

4. WHAT IF: (10% 3-5min)

Objections and responses (1-3):

O1:_____

R1: _____

O2:_____

R2: _____

O3:_____

R3: _____

3 actions the reader should take as a result of reading this chapter:

1._____

2._____

3._____

Additional information/resources:

_____

_____

_____

_____

_____

_____

_____

'How to' Style Book – Chapter Unpack Template

Chapter Name: _____

Opening Sentence:

_____

_____

_____

1. WHY: (Start Here) **(25% 5-7min)**

1. _____
2. _____
3. _____
4. _____
5. _____

Fact/Statistic/Shocking truth (1):

_____

_____

Quotes (2): Google relevant quotesfor this chapter.

Contrast/Pain (1):

_____

_____

2. WHAT: **(5% 1min)** Define each term

_____

_____

_____

_____

_____

_____

_____

3. HOW: (60% 10-12mins)

3 different ways to teach the WHAT using Stories to illustrate it...

1._____

_____

2._____

_____

3._____

_____

4. WHAT IF: (10% 3-5min)

Objections and responses (1-3):

O1:_____

R1:_____

O2:_____

R2:_____

O3:_____

R3:_____

3 actions the reader should take as a result of reading this chapter:

1._____

2._____

3._____

Additional information/resources:

_____

_____

_____

_____

_____

_____

'How to' Style Book – Chapter Unpack Template

Chapter Name: _____

Opening Sentence:

_____

_____

_____

1. WHY: (Start Here) **(25% 5-7min)**

1. _____

2. _____

3. _____

4. _____

5. _____

Fact/Statistic/Shocking truth (1):

_____

_____

Quotes (2): Google relevant quotesfor this chapter.

Contrast/Pain (1):

_____

_____

2. WHAT: (5% 1min) Define each term

_____

_____

_____

_____

_____

_____

_____

_____

3. HOW: (60% 10-12mins)

3 different ways to teach the WHAT using Stories to illustrate it...

1._____

_____

2._____

_____

3._____

_____

4. WHAT IF: (10% 3-5min)

Objections and responses (1-3):

O1:_____

R1: _____

O2:_____

R2: _____

O3: _____

R3: _____

3 actions the reader should take as a result of reading this chapter:

1._____

2._____

3._____

Additional information/resources:

_____

_____

_____

_____

_____

_____

_____

'How to' Style Book – Chapter Unpack Template

Chapter Name: _____

Opening Sentence:

_____

_____

_____

1. WHY: (Start Here) **(25% 5-7min)**

1. _____

2. _____

3. _____

4. _____

5. _____

Fact/Statistic/Shocking truth (1):

_____

_____

Quotes (2): Google relevant quotesfor this chapter.

Contrast/Pain (1):

_____

_____

2. WHAT: **(5% 1min)** Define each term

_____

_____

_____

_____

_____

_____

_____

_____

3. HOW: (60% 10-12mins)

3 different ways to teach the WHAT using Stories to illustrate it...

1._____

_____

2._____

_____

3._____

_____

4. WHAT IF: (10% 3-5min)

Objections and responses (1-3):

O1:_____

R1: _____

O2:_____

R2: _____

O3:_____

R3: _____

3 actions the reader should take as a result of reading this chapter:

1._____

2._____

3._____

Additional information/resources:

_____

_____

_____

_____

_____

_____

_____

PREP CHECKLIST

Before our authors come away to their Ultimate 48 Hour Author retreat, we ask them to complete this checklist. It normally takes 10-12 hours of preparation in order to be ready for the execution of their content. Whether the author will speak out or type out their book, this is essential. It removes any writer's block and fast tracks the whole process.

48 Hour Author Pre-Weekend Checklist

- ☐ Be clear on your Purpose for the book
- ☐ Be clear on the Target Market & the Problem
- ☐ Book Title and Tagline chosen
- ☐ All Chapters and Sexy Names for them outlined
- ☐ All Chapters Unpacked
- ☐ Plan for your Introduction and Afterword
- ☐ Create a 3D Mock-up Cover
- ☐ Thoughts around the design of Book Cover (Amazon)
- ☐ Collect 5-10 Testimonials from clients or book content related
- ☐ Think about a Dedication for your book
- ☐ Come up with your 3 Programmes/Offers that will go at the back
- ☐ Write your bio – About the Author (200-700 words)
- ☐ Write the Blurb for the Back of the Book (150 words)
- ☐ Choose any Quotes you may like to include relevant to chapters
- ☐ Set up your Dropbox, IngramSpark, and Amazon accounts
- ☐ If you want to have Illustrations/Diagrams, get them organised beforehand

In the following pages are some templates for most of the sections of the prep checklist. They will guide you as to what you need to include and how to think about them. Take time to then fill out the content or at the very least some bullet points so that you can use those to type them up properly in your manuscript.

INTRODUCTION

Bullet Point your shorthand notes to unpack what you will say in the Introduction. Make sure you address the following as a guide. You may like to do it below here:

1. Who is the book's intended audience?

_____

_____

_____

_____

_____

_____

2. Why you wrote the book.

_____

_____

_____

_____

_____

_____

3. How the reader can use the book.

_____

_____

_____

_____

_____

_____

4. A short summary story around what inspired you to put it out there – is there a story that prompted you, or a moment you knew you had to share what they are about to read?

_____

_____

_____

_____

_____

_____

_____

_____

_____

_____

AFTERWORD

Bullet Point your short-hand notes to unpack what you will say in the Afterword. This part of the book is a quick summary, or as I like to say, a pep talk of congratulating the reader for completing the book and perhaps what they can do now that they have finished.

Do you want them to go back through it and do the exercises suggested, how do you encourage them to go forward, etc. ...?

_____

_____

_____

_____

_____

_____

_____

_____

_____

_____

_____

_____

_____

_____

_____

_____

_____

_____

_____

DEDICATION

This is a single sentence of to whom you want to dedicate the book. It can be family, children, the reader, clients, or someone who has made an impact on your life. This is your personal choice, anything goes that feels right for you.

_____

_____

_____

_____

_____

_____

_____

_____

_____

_____

_____

_____

ABOUT THE AUTHOR

Usually 200-700 words. This is written in the 3rd person. It is your professional Bio with all your contact details at the end. It's recommended that you put an author photo here. How to structure this section...

1. Write a little on your history, upbringing, family (humanise).

_____

_____

_____

_____

_____

2. Write about your professional qualifications and current activities.

_____

_____

_____

_____

_____

3. Write about your passion for the future and the difference you want to make.

_____

_____

_____

_____

_____

4. Finish with your contact details, email and websites.

_____

_____

_____

_____

_____

BLURB

The second thing people will judge your book on (after your front cover) will be what is written on the back cover of the book. Make this section 150-200 words in length as it will need to fit on the back cover without looking too busy. This should be written in the 3rd person. It needs to be sexy and sell the magic bullet to the reader so they are excited and drawn to read the book.

Use language that will sell an easy step-by-step system / formula / blueprint, the changes they will experience while reading the book, how easy and effortless it will be. And really address that the problem they may be having now which they are aware of will vanish after they have picked up the insights / strategies / tools shared in the book.

_____

_____

_____

_____

_____

_____

_____

_____

_____

_____

_____

_____

_____

_____

_____

_____

_____

COVER DESIGN

If you intend to position your personal brand and business brand and be recognised as the face behind the voice of the book, I strongly recommend that you have an image of yourself on the cover. This is especially important for coaches, consultants, speakers and practitioners.

Check out other covers on Amazon and come up with ideas for yourself. E.g., full body shot, portrait, any props you might use, what you will wear. Wear solid colours as they are less distracting and will look great on the cover.

Also consider the following checklist I use when designing book covers:

- ☐ Use a sans serif (clean font) that is easy to read. Avoid curly fonts unless that is your preference

- ☐ The title should be as big as possible on the cover so it can be easily read on a thumbnail on Amazon and other online platforms

- ☐ Wherever possible use colours that make the cover pop

- ☐ Match colours to your image or branding for more consistency

- ☐ Remember to place your logo and website on the back cover

- ☐ Work with the idea of 'less is more'

- ☐ Make sure the tagline does not look too cluttered if it's long – never make a tagline go across 3-4 lines; 1-2 is the maximum

- ☐ Consider if there are special fonts you would like to see – let your designer know before they start the design process.

YOUR BOOK COVER IDEAS AND SAMPLES

Use this page to jot down some ideas for your book cover in line with what you read on the previous page. You may also like to print some covers off the internet to show your designer a style you would like. The more info and guidance you have, the faster you will get to your vision with the designer. You may also choose to have them come up with a few concepts and go from there.

_____

_____

_____

_____

_____

_____

_____

_____

_____

_____

_____

_____

_____

_____

_____

_____

_____

_____

_____

_____

_____

_____

TESTIMONIALS

Here are important guidelines for your testimonials:

- They go at the start of your book and before your offers at the back

- Keep them short: 2-3 sentences per testimonial. Picking the best bits that others have said, will have the most impact

- Get permission from the people – via email is ok

- If you don't have client testimonials, people who know you well can give you a character reference

- Always put the person's name and position on the testimonial

- Look out for credible people who may be able to give you a testimonial; if it's someone very influential, put the testimonial on the cover (the most powerful statement)

- If you can't get all 10, it's ok; 5-8 will do as well.

Please Note:

If you haven't had clients before or are not allowed to have client testimonials for your business (e.g., Chiropractors, psychologists, etc.), then when your book is in editing, you can give the draft copy to people you trust. Give them either the full book or a few chapters and get them to give you a testimonial on the book content. Again, even 5 testimonials will be sufficient.

ACKNOWLEDGEMENTS

Are there some people that helped you during the authoring process?
Would you like to give thanks to someone special. Use this section to jot
down those you would like to remember to thank. You can make this as
short or long as you like. It can be from one sentence to one page.

_____

_____

_____

_____

_____

_____

_____

_____

_____

_____

_____

_____

_____

_____

_____

_____

_____

_____

_____

_____

_____

_____

_____

_____

_____

BOOK LAYOUT DOCUMENT

(Submit to Editing by following the guidelines below)

DO:

- Submit Only Text as Your Manuscript (in Doc file format Microsoft WORD NOT Pages, which is the Mac word processor) Editors do not use any other word processing software but Word

- Cut and Paste everything in allocated areas by following the order below – you must be working on one single file

- Put all the titles on your chapters, sections and subsections

- Type in Image Name or Diagram/Illustration Name in Red where it needs to appear in the manuscript e.g. Insert Image DSC4532 Here

Style suggestions:

- Start each section on a new page by using Control Enter (apple computers Command Enter)

- Font – Calibri 12 for the body

- Chapter Headings 14 Bold Centred (e.g. Chapter 2 – Sexy Chapter Title) and BOLD use of sub headings in chapters

- Quotes in Italic and centred

- Bullet points consistent throughout

- Even spacing between paragraphs

DON'T

- Create a Contents Page, Title Page or Copyright page – it is done by the designer at layout for you

- Include any images or illustrations in your word document

CUT & PASTE YOUR CONTENT BELOW IN ALLOCATED AREAS:

1. Paste in Testimonials Below (optional and only if you want to)

2. Paste in Dedication Below

3. Paste in Preface or Foreword (optional – not many do it)

4. Paste in Introduction Below

5. Paste in all your Chapters in Order Below

6. Paste in any Appendices Below, Optional for graphs, checklists, tables (if tables submit separately for designer to create and put in for you)

7. Paste in About the Author Below (written in the 3rd person)

8. Paste in your Acknowledgements section (optional but many have done it)

9. Paste in more Testimonials (optional)

10. Paste in Your 3 Offers with Calls to Action Below

11. Put in any Sponsor or Affiliate Adverts Below (Optional – only done very rarely) – if images just type in what image goes there and submit images separately

12. Paste in your Blurb for the back of your book (written in the 3rd person)

Note: For Images/Diagrams/Illustrations it's best to create one Dropbox Folder and put all in there – we will share this folder with your layout designer and they will be able to match up the name of the image to where it needs to go as specified.

POST WEEKEND CHECKLIST

Following our Ultimate 48 Hour Author Retreats, we give our authors the following checklist. Here I will give you some ideas and tips on how to execute it for yourself.

- ☐ Complete the transcription of your audios
- ☐ Finalise your full cover design
- ☐ Keep executing your pre-launch campaign
- ☐ Create a sales landing page if you have not already done so
- ☐ Laminate your book cover to take around everywhere you go
- ☐ Finalise any sections in the book that are not being transcribed
- ☐ Cut and paste everything in order using the book layout document
- ☐ Buy a self-publishing package to execute the publishing process professionally
- ☐ When your book goes to print start planning your book launch party

KEY 3 - LEVERAGE

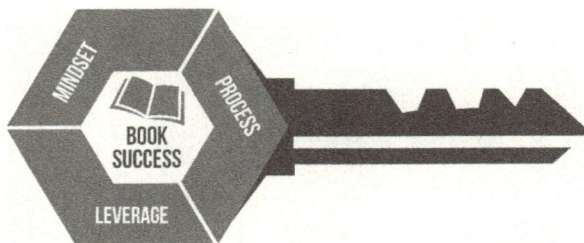

YOUR OFFERS

If your intention with your book is to generate more business and find new clients, you need to provide the next steps your reader can take with you, in order to get involved at a deeper level to help solve their problem.

Offers can vary from Free to High-End. I recommend you have a range of Free, Low-Cost and High-End options. The power of three is usually best. Do not put any prices on your offers as these may change as time goes by. The only time I would suggest putting a price on is if an offer is low-cost and something you would always be happy to run at that price point to attract more potential clients into your business.

If you are writing your book as a personal story, you may not have multiple offers at the back of the book. However, every author can have their Speaker Bio as part of that section of the book.

Here are some ideas on what you can create as your offers if you are starting from scratch and writing a 'How to' book:

- Downloadable free eBook that is further value in addition to your book content – this is great to get leads into your sales funnel and communicate with them to build rapport and a relationship. It's been said that people need to consume 10-12 hours of your content before they are ready to buy from you

- Checklists, templates or questionnaires that would help the reader on the topic they are consuming
- Audio or Video resource
- Free Mini Online Course
- Introductory consultation at low-cost
- Calls to action to join an online community/group
- Group Mastermind programme
- Membership option (low or high-end)
- One on One Consulting/Coaching packages
- Online course
- Retreats
- Shorter Workshops
- Master classes
- Done for you packages
- Your Speaker Bio/Profile
- 30-day Challenge if you plan to run it regularly

Key Steps when Advertising Your Offers at the Back of Your Book

All offers need to be compelling and attractive for the reader to want to take the next step and get further help. They need to really help fill the next gap for the person reading the book who has the problem you can help them solve.

To make offers appealing, always add a visual aspect to them. Think about what would be a relevant image to match the offer.

Examples include: Consulting session (image of you consulting someone), Speaker Bio (you speaking in front of a group of people), eBook (3D mock up cover image of the eBook), Online course (image of a computer screen with your course on the screen)

Next is the copy. Remember the hypnotic words? This is where you will need to use many and attract the reader at their pain points and wants to make that pain go away. Use questions, bullet points and hypnotic headlines or names for your offers to have the most impact.

Lastly have a call to action. How does the reader find out more? Is there a limit to your offer? For example: We only give away 5 of these consulting sessions each month. Contact us to find out if you can have yours this month.

Take time to check out the offers towards the back of this planner so that you can see what I mean.

Now over to you – I am giving you five templates to start brainstorming and playing with your offers. Don't stress if you have not created something yet and you are advertising it. By the time your book is out and someone wants it, you will very quickly find the time and space to deliver on your promise – this is what I call the cure to procrastination! Make a commitment to someone else first and then go into creation mode when they have requested it from you. So long as you know it's all in your head, you can get it out easily when the pressure is on.

HOT TIP: If you have a free offer as a lead magnet, mention it in the introduction. This way if someone downloads the sample of your book on Amazon and doesn't buy your book after that, if they are enjoying it and see the bonus offer, they may end up downloading it. This means you will get their contact details and will be able to communicate and build a relationship with them as well as your database list.

OFFER CREATION TEMPLATE

Type of offer: _____

Price point: _____

Sexy/Hypnotic Name of Offer: _____

Image that would match the offer: _____

Questions I could ask to sell the offer:

Pain Q: _____

Pain Q: _____

Pleasure Q: _____

3-5 Key Sexy/Hypnotic Benefits of the offer:

- _____

- _____

- _____

- _____

- _____

Call to action: _____

_____

OFFER CREATION TEMPLATE

Type of offer: _____

Price point: _____

Sexy/Hypnotic Name of Offer: _____

Image that would match the offer: _____

Questions I could ask to sell the offer:

Pain Q: _____

Pain Q: _____

Pleasure Q: _____

3-5 Key Sexy/Hypnotic Benefits of the offer:

- _____

- _____

- _____

- _____

- _____

Call to action: _____

_____

OFFER CREATION TEMPLATE

Type of offer: _____

Price point: _____

Sexy/Hypnotic Name of Offer: _____

Image that would match the offer: _____

Questions I could ask to sell the offer:

Pain Q: _____

Pain Q: _____

Pleasure Q: _____

3-5 Key Sexy/Hypnotic Benefits of the offer:

- _____

- _____

- _____

- _____

- _____

Call to action: _____

_____

OFFER CREATION TEMPLATE

Type of offer: _____

Price point: _____

Sexy/Hypnotic Name of Offer: _____

Image that would match the offer: _____

Questions I could ask to sell the offer:

Pain Q: _____

Pain Q: _____

Pleasure Q: _____

3-5 Key Sexy/Hypnotic Benefits of the offer:

- _____

- _____

- _____

- _____

- _____

Call to action: _____

_____

OFFER CREATION TEMPLATE

Type of offer: _____

Price point: _____

Sexy/Hypnotic Name of Offer: _____

Image that would match the offer: _____

Questions I could ask to sell the offer:

Pain Q: _____

Pain Q: _____

Pleasure Q: _____

3-5 Key Sexy/Hypnotic Benefits of the offer:

- _____

- _____

- _____

- _____

- _____

Call to action: _____

_____

SPEAKER BIO

Natasa Denman is The Ultimate 48 Hour Author. A highly sought after professional speaker (CSP accredited - Certified Speaking Professional), Natasa is a 7 times published author and creator of the game changing business model, Ultimate 48 Hour Author. She has helped over 150 small business owners become first time published authors in just 3 years.

In 6 short years in business, Natasa has been nominated for The Telstra Businesswoman of the Year twice and was a finalist in AusMumpreneur of the Year in Product Innovation.

Appearing in all major media outlets across Australia, Natasa is changing the way people do business in Australia and now runs a 7-figure business with her husband and 3 children travelling the country, spreading her message and helping small businesses thrive.

Ultimate 48 Hour Author Blueprint for Business Success

- How to Leverage Your Business via a Book
- Lucratively Position Your Book for Success
- How to write a book in Just 48 Hours

Ultimate Brand Accelerator Formula

- How to Stand out and Thrive in Your Industry
- Hi-Touch, Hi-Tech and Hi-Fame Strategies
- The One thing that will Fast Track Your Following

1000 Days to a Million Dollar Coaching Business from Home

- How to build infrastructure for a 7 figure business
- Marketing Smarts to keep your Pipeline full
- Sales Mastery Insider Tactics

📞 +61 412 085 160 | ✉ natasa@natasadenman.com | 🌐 www.natasadenman.com

Speaker Bios are so powerful to have and use online and offline. My speaker bio has gotten me so many speaking gigs and opportunities as it gives organisers a clear picture of who I am, what I can speak on and what the audience will learn as a result of listening to me. It is also important you have this designed professionally, so that you can print it off and give it to those who are looking for speakers. There are five key aspects to think about when creating your speaker bio:

1. Your Sexy/Hypnotic personal bio

2. Your Sexy/Hypnotic keynote topics (3 in total)

3. Your Sexy/Hypnotic takeaway points (3 per topic)

4. Your Credibility Images

5. Your Contact details

Here is a Template for you to fill out to start pulling all of this together.

SPEAKER BIO TEMPLATE

Re-write your About the Author bio down to 100-120 words. Use the best and most credible parts of what you have achieved thus far. You are looking to present a star profile. Use my example earlier as a guide. Don't be too shy to let yourself shine.

_____
_____
_____
_____
_____
_____
_____
_____
_____
_____

Sexy/Hypnotic Keynote topics:

1. _____

2. _____

3. _____

Sexy/Hypnotic takeaway points for each keynote topic:

TOPIC 1: _____

- _____
- _____
- _____

TOPIC 2: _____

- _____
- _____
- _____

TOPIC 3: _____

- _____
- _____
- _____

Credibility Images you will use in the design of your Speaker Bio:

- ☐ Professional photo of you
- ☐ Your logo
- ☐ You speaking in front of an audience
- ☐ Your book cover
- ☐ Media logos

You do not need all of the above, just what you can come up with. Ensure they are in high resolution. Once done with the above send all the details to a designer to pull together your awesome Speaker Bio. Update your Bio every 1-2 years or more frequently if things are changing for you. Put your Speaker Bio amongst the offers at the back of the book.

MARKETING IDEAS FOR YOUR BOOK

Writing a book is one thing, making money from it is a completely new skill set you will need to develop and refine. Testing and measuring will become your friend and you will get out of it what you put in. Move as far away as possible from the idea that you will get rich just selling books. The money is not in the books, but in the leverage you create with your content. That is exactly why I recommend you have your offers and calls to action at the back of the book.

Even with no offers advertised, I was able to build a six-figure business with my very first book within twelve months of its release. How did I do that? Here are the exact actions I took:

- Went networking twice a week the previous twelve months and developed a network of people who knew me, liked me and trusted me.

- Whenever someone asked for a speaker for their group or event, I would put my hand up no matter how scared I was.

- I ran my own events initially with 5-10 people per event at best.

- I looked and created a couple of key joint ventures with others who had my target market. At the time my topic was weight loss coaching, so I did this with a couple of chiropractors and personal training studio owners.

- I shared daily about my journey on Facebook, my main social media platform

- I created crappy videos to promote the launch of the book (even though at the time I thought they were good)

- I connected with my list (database) minimum weekly to add value and further nurture the relationships.

- I always had a call to action!!! (This is a huge one that many fail at as they don't want to appear salesy. You need to tell people what you want them to do; they can't read your mind!!!)

I did many other things that did not work, but I am only sharing with you what did. I stuck to consistent routines in all this and it certainly paid off big time in launching my book and business from 3 clients in the first twelve months to a fully booked coaching practice in the next twelve.

Now over to you. What will you commit to with consistency to promote your book and your business? List at least 5 actions you will take regularly to become visible:

1. _____
2. _____
3. _____
4. _____
5. _____
6. _____
7. _____

BBQ SPEECH

The first places I got noticed in business and was able to start monetizing my business was at networking events. To this day being able to answer the question 'What do you do?' powerfully, brings in so much interest and many clients. The absolute secret to being able to gain a prospective client's interest quickly is to appear valuable to them, to appear as though you may be able to get them something they want.

To achieve that end you need to develop your BBQ speech, which you will use when introducing yourself or when asked what you do (as might happen at a BBQ, or at a brief business encounter). To have that, you need first to have clear and concise answers to the following 5 questions:

A. With whom do you seek to do business?

_____

_____

_____

B. What are their 3 biggest and most critical problems?

1._____

2._____

3._____

C. How do you solve those problems – uniquely?

_____

_____

_____

_____

_____

_____

_____

D. Include a client's most dramatic (WOW!) results.

_____

_____

_____

E. List the deepest benefits your clients gain & how they feel about those.

_____

_____

_____

Your BBQ Speech

Now let's put together your BBQ Speech, which will always take the following form:

1. You know how (answer to A.) do, are, or feel (answer to B.)?

2. Well, what I do is (answer to C.)

3. The result is (answer to D.)

4. The benefits are (lots of answers E.)

Let's try that:

You know how

_____

_____

_____

do, are, or feel

_____

_____

_____

Well, what I do is

_____

_____

_____

The result is

_____
_____
_____

One of my recent clients

_____
_____
_____
_____
_____

An Example

You know how a lot of business owners find themselves overloaded with work and people issues and often with tight cash flow, and can feel stressed and on the edge of control a lot of the time? Well, I use some really simple systems to lower their workload, improve their leadership, free up their cash flow and create new profits. You'd be amazed at how much different those clients look and how differently they feel after just 6 months.

One of my recent clients who, even with 32 staff was still generating 60% of her company's sales, has changed all of that. Last week she came back from a three-week cruise and told me that she was training her staff for her five-week cruise starting next month. Sales are up, profits are up – and she's no longer responsible for any sales. She looks about 10 years younger and reckons she feels it too.

Putting Your BBQ Speech into Practice

Rehearse this until it's totally natural and you'll be fascinating to everyone and of huge interest to the right people, or to anyone who knows and cares about people who would benefit from making your acquaintance.

Once you have your hook into their "interest nerve" turn on your Active Listening, ask lots of questions about them, and you're going to look like the most interesting genius they've met this year! Your social challenges are over!

ADVANCED MARKETING STRATEGIES

Once you have a bit of a marketing budget behind you, you can start playing a bigger game. I certainly don't think you should jump into paid advertising if you have not in some way monetised what you do. Completing and doing the steps I did with my first book will easily help you confirm that you can both monetise your niche and that you have the expertise needed (that is if you haven't confirmed it already).

When you have certainty that your model is one that you can scale, paid advertising is the way to go. Here are the strategies I execute nowadays to leverage my business and books:

- Run 35 half day workshops in a year, advertising them on Facebook to get bums on seats. This event has been finetuned, refined and tested, and provides $1.5 million in revenue for us a year. We sell our online portal, books, planners and retreat programme

- I still continue to implement some of my organic strategies to get bums on seats and speak at events for free to attract more people into my half day workshop

- Run 3 x two-day master classes with another influential joint venture partner that has my ideal audience. I bring her new clients and she does the same for me as we both advertise and get new people into our business regularly. We also both end up adding value to each others' clients, and at the very least starting some new relationships and expanding our visibility.

- I get asked many times to be interviewed on podcasts, radio and for other collaborative partners' clients

- I have been a major sponsor four times for the speakers association and the global speakers summit. This is how I met my UAE partner and expanded the business internationally.

Being able to reinvest in my business has seen it grow exponentially to a point that we ended up opening our in-house publishing company and hiring more people to help us run it. When you find the things that work like magic (the good news is, you can find the top 3) you will be able to have laser sharp focus and the ability to replicate your results consistently and with great success.

A lot of the time I find people write books because they are after a certain lifestyle. This is truly possible. I am proof that it can happen with some hard work in the early years and then clever decision making on what to keep doing and what no longer serves you or is keeping you busy for the sake of being busy.

We chose this to be a lifestyle business, having four month off over a year travelling the world with our kids, and enjoying the rewards from the hard work we put in at the other times. We have intense periods of lots of events and periods when we are setting up new systems and structures so things run even more smoothly in the future.

In the following two pages, document what you would like your book and business to do for your life. Use details, specifics and visions of what your life will be like when you are a successful author.

_____

_____

_____

_____

_____

_____

_____

_____

_____

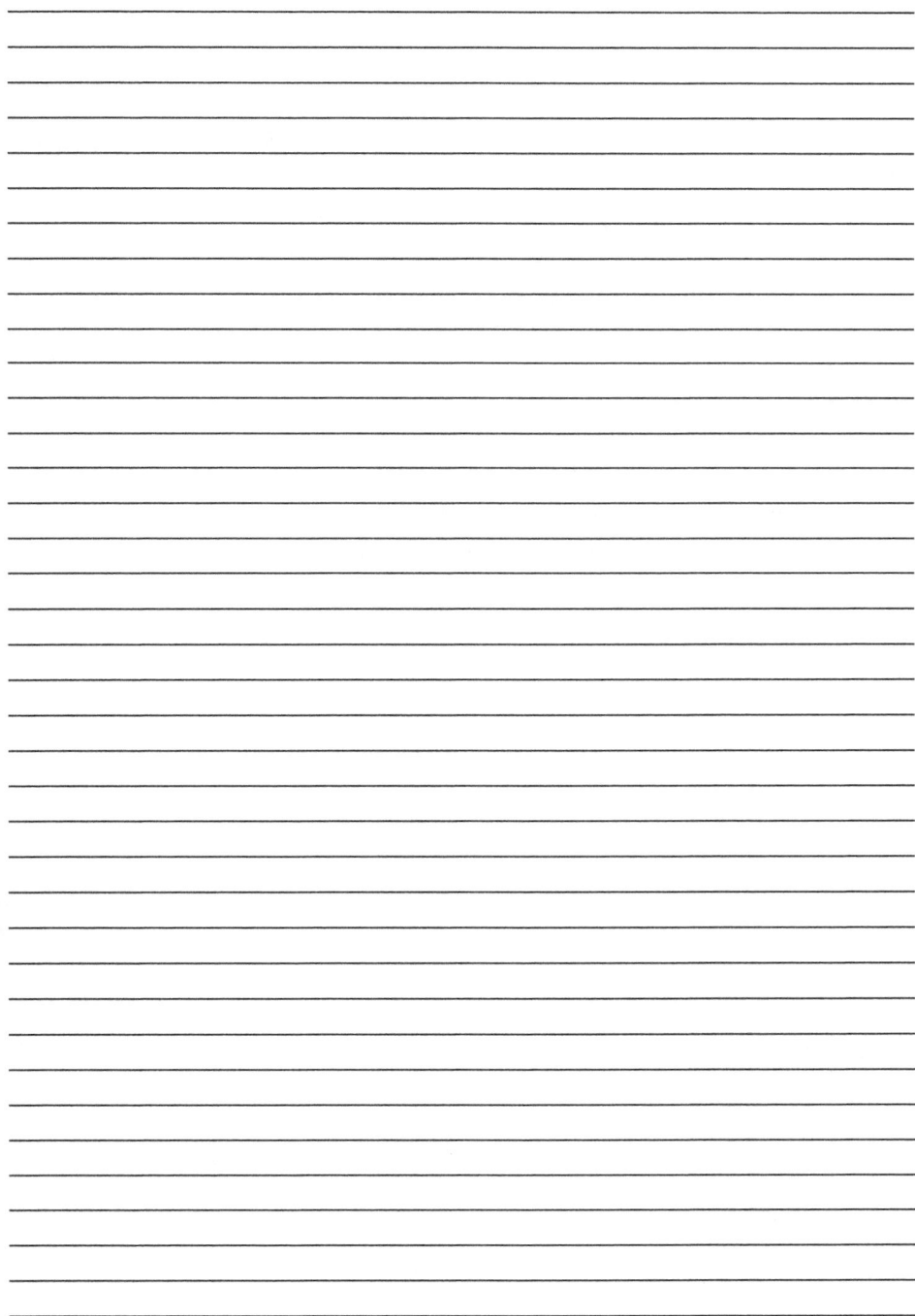

CREATING A SIMPLE BOOK WEBSITE

Having somewhere to send your interested readers is essential to your book success. You will come across as professional and make the ordering process super easy. You can go for an elaborate website or you can simply create a book landing page that will be able to process sales for you. You will then be able to use this in all your promotions online and offline.

If you are not savvy with websites, don't do it yourself. Landing pages don't need to cost a lot of money. You can find someone via Upwork.com to do something like this for around the $100 mark. When you do find someone, make sure that you instruct them clearly and provide them with all the information they need. Here is your checklist of things you will need to give them:

- ☐ Your Name
- ☐ Website URL (the domain name you have bought – I recommend that you buy your name.com and your book name.com)
- ☐ Login details for your hosting company. This is the place you bought your domain – you will also need to buy hosting of the website
- ☐ Logo – send the designer in high resolution
- ☐ Preferred colours and/or fonts
- ☐ Your book cover in high resolution
- ☐ Sale price of book
- ☐ PayPal details if that is the way you will take payments
- ☐ Your book blurb
- ☐ Any other benefits about your book

- ☐ Short About the Author section
- ☐ Photo of you in high resolution
- ☐ Social media links
- ☐ Video link if you are embedding video on the page

Remember to remain patient during the design process of your website and communicate clearly. Use of sketches and screenshot videos can work well for a more visual explanation if you feel your designer is not understanding you.

Want to do it yourself?

Here are a few platforms you can check out to build this yourself:

- Strikingly.com (free if you use their domain which will include the word strikingly or around $100 for your own domain and annual hosting – I use this for my natasadenman.com website)
- Clickfunnels.com (monthly subscription unlimited landing page templates you can choose from and build)
- Leadpages.com (monthly subscription unlimited landing page templates you can choose from and build)
- Wix.com

YOUR BOOK LAUNCH

Here is a quick checklist on what you need to consider when planning your book launch:

- ☐ Paid or not paid (2 hours length)
- ☐ Choosing a venue, is there parking, how central is it?
- ☐ How will you set it up – decorations to match your book theme
- ☐ If you will run Video and need Audio as with over 40 people you will need a microphone
- ☐ Professional Photographer/Videographer
- ☐ Times food will come out
- ☐ Crew – especially at registration (how many do you need?)
- ☐ Door Prizes from you and sponsors
- ☐ Will you have an MC?
- ☐ Will you have sponsors and other speakers?
- ☐ How will you structure your speech – will you be interviewed or make a speech?
- ☐ Music
- ☐ Drink and book vouchers
- ☐ Pre-signing the message in your books so you then only personalise them, so it's quicker
- ☐ Logistics emails before and after Launch
- ☐ Registration Process
- ☐ Arrive at venue 2 hours before the event so you are set up with 1 hr to go and can relax and have a drink
- ☐ Change into your good clothes once set up and take flats with you if you intend to wear high heels for the rest of the launch.

FREE BONUS

Life truly changes when you become a first-time author. Recently we interviewed many of our authors on their journeys, and the experience for each of them has been slightly different and very interesting even for us to explore. So I created this amazing bonus to the book, so that you can deep dive into the mindset and experience of a first-time author.

Here are some of the questions we asked:

- What is your book about and why did you write it?
- What was your biggest challenge when deciding to write your first book?
- Who were your biggest doubters and has their opinion changed now that you are published?
- Why did you decide to do the Ultimate 48 Hour Author program for your first book?
- What advice would you give a first-time author?
- What has happened now that your book is out?
- Will you be writing more books in the future?

Simply go to the link below and download your copy instantly:
bit.ly/shutupfreeebook

ULTIMATE 48 HOUR AUTHOR ONLINE PORTAL

The Ultimate 48 Hour Author Online Portal is a fully ONLINE Do It Yourself (DIY) programme that combines the Ultimate 48 Hour Blueprint as well as everything you need to complete your first book to the point of having a manuscript ready to go into publishing.

It has been fully customised to include not only the U48A Online Course, but four other super valuable resources to help you reach completion and keep you supported along the way.

We have had authors in four different countries write and publish their books using our Online Portal as they utilised the various inclusions to maximise their results in the shortest possible time.

Like all online programmes, the onus is on you to work through the provided content and make a commitment to completion, not to just buy this and put it on the shelf (or leave it sit on your computer).

If writing your book is important to you and you are unable to join our signature all-inclusive Ultimate 48 Hour Author Retreat programme, our Online Portal is a great place to start as you can always upgrade into our retreat programme within 12 months of commencing this programme.

There are five key components that make up the sum of the Online Portal.

- Ultimate 48 Hour Author Online Course
- Bums on Seats Online Course
- Access to the Full Training Footage of seminars Natasa Denman has run
- Weekly Q&A Live Calls in the Ultimate 48 Hour Author Mastermind Community
- Access to exclusive Members Only Author Facebook Community

Here is a more detailed description of each component:

1. Ultimate 48 Hour Author Online Course

12 x 30 min modules - The Complete Ultimate 48 Hour Author Blueprint

Includes

- Online course delivered via 12 video modules
- Checklists
- Templates

Doesn't Include

- One-on-one mentoring
- Custom review of your work
- Email support
- Publishing, design or transcription (including editing, layout, printing, etc.)

2. Bums on Seats Online Course

Includes

- Online course delivered via 12 video modules
- Checklists
- Templates

Doesn't Include

- One-on-one mentoring
- Custom feedback on your work

3. Access to the Full Training Footage from Natasa Denman

Includes

- Social Media Masterclass
- Sales Mastery Masterclass
- Bums on Seats Masterclass
- Publicity Training
- Running Webinars for Profit and much, much, more (approx. 200 hours in total)

48 Hour Authors Private   Speak for Profit Masterclass   Dubai U48A Retreat Jan 2018   Sales Mastery Mastermind
   Feb 2018   2017

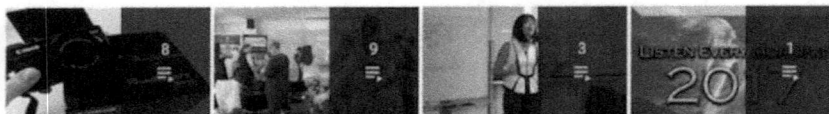

Liked videos   Social Media Masterclass   Blueprint for Ultimate Book   Ester Hicks
   March 2017   Writing Success Workshop

City Events   Sales Mastery Masterclass   Interviews with Ultimate 48   Retreat Nov 2016 Teach
   July 17 Melbourne   Hour Authors   Sessions

4. Weekly Q&A Live Calls in the Ultimate 48 Hour Author Mastermind Community

Jump on the Monday morning Live Calls with Nat at 9:30am Melbourne time to ask all your burning questions as you are completing your manuscript. These are recorded and you can access them via a link that will be provided to you.

5. Author Only Secret Online Community

Mastermind with other published and soon to be published authors.

Includes

- Support from authors in front of you or on your journey
- Ask questions and get instant feedback
- Network with potential joint venture opportunties

You can upgrade to retreat within 12 months of joining the Online Portal. The other option is to complete the Online Portal and request a Publishing Only quote for your manuscript.

Contact us to discuss your suitability on 1300 664 006.

BOOK PUBLISHING ONLY

ULTIMATE WORLD
—— PUBLISHING ——

If self-publishing your book is your only requirement, we can help.

Introducing Ultimate World Publishing – the publishing company that wants nothing more but to help you get your book in your hands with full control of everything.

We promise that you will:

- Receive your print ready files with no strings attached

- Be able to control the number of copies and timing of the publishing of your book as it will be on your own print on demand account

- Never be sold expensive marketing done-for-you packages as we don't offer them

- Get your book done super-fast (after all we run the Ultimate 48 Hour Author!)

- Have one dedicated team member work with you during your book publishing project

- Get to keep all your profits and royalties as we want to set you free after we help you with your book

- Have access to our amazing secret community of over 300 authors (so far).

Quoting on book publishing is difficult without a conversation. Specifics such as the size of the book, style of paper, colour, images and product finish vary the cost significantly from book to book.

Our **Ultimate Publishing Package** includes the following as standard:

- ISBN numbers for both your book and ebook

- Copyediting

- Proofing of your book by our editor post internal layout

- Professional print ready cover design

- Full internal layout of up to 15 images included

- Ebook conversion of your book

- Amazon upload of your book

- Print on demand upload and set up via IngramSpark

- One proof print copy of your book

- One lot of revised files re-uploaded to IngramSpark upon reviewing your book

- Australian National and State Library deposit of your book.

Call us for a 10-minute chat on 1300 664 006 or fill out the inquiry form on our website www.writeabook.com.au/ultimateworld-publishing/ so we can determine what your vision is for your book. We'll then provide a quote on a customised package that will enable you to publish a book that is the perfect reflection of your style, brand and personality.

Ultimate 48 Hour Author Packages

	Done For You Retreat	Do It Yourself
Online Author Portal	✓	✓
Ultimate 48 Hour Author online course (12 modules + resources)	✓	✓
Weekly Q&A Live Calls in Secret Author's Group	✓	✓
Bums on Seats online course (12 modules + resources)	✓	✓
Library of over 200 hours of filmed footage on marketing & sales	✓	✓
Lifetime membership to our Secret Facebook Communities	✓	✓
Mentoring & Accountability	✓	
2 Hour pre-weekend prep session one on one	✓	
Unlimited email support	✓	
Laser mentoring until book release	✓	
Success Modules:	✓	
1. Leverage via Further Products	✓	
2. The Power of Social Media	✓	
3. Connecting Through Video	✓	
4. Free Publicity Generation	✓	
5. Automation Savvy	✓	
6. Pre-Launch Campaign	✓	
7. Your Mindset Success	✓	
8. Transcription of Your Book - 5 Hours Max	✓	
9. Checklists, Templates & Guides for Your Success	✓	
Retreat Package	✓	
Luxury accommodation – 2 nights	✓	
Restaurant style meals	✓	
Publishing Package	✓	
ISBN/Barcode for both book and ebook	✓	
Copyediting and proofing (40 000 words max)	✓	
Internal layout & design (15 images total included)	✓	
Mock-up cover creation for pre-launch	✓	
Professional final cover design	✓	
300 books (colour cover, black and white internal printing)	✓	
Ebook version of your book	✓	
Amazon upload of your book	✓	
IngramSpark upload print on demand set up	✓	
National and state library deposit	✓	
Online Masterclasses (6 Days per Year)	✓	
Speak for Profit (9-5)	✓	
Social Media (9-5)	✓	
Bums on Seats (9-5)	✓	
Products for Profit (9-5)	✓	
Technology & Marketing (9-5)	✓	
Sales Mastery (9-5)		

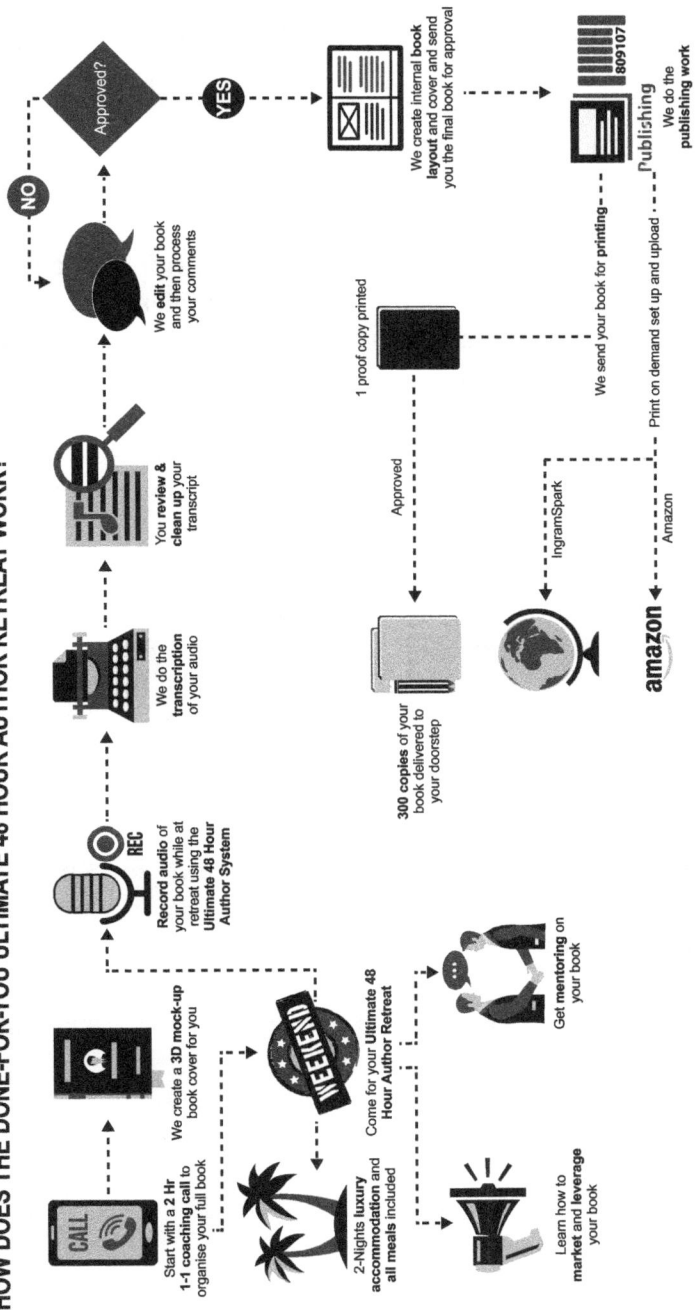

GO AWAY ON A RETREAT, COME BACK AS AN AUTHOR HOLD YOUR BOOK IN YOUR HANDS WITHIN MONTHS

ULTIMATE 48 HOUR AUTHOR

HOW DOES THE DONE-FOR-YOU ULTIMATE 48 HOUR AUTHOR RETREAT WORK?

Start with a 2 Hr 1-1 **coaching** call to organise your full book

We create a **3D mock-up** book cover for you

WEEKEND

Come for your **Ultimate 48 Hour Author Retreat**

2-Nights **luxury accommodation** and all meals included

Get **mentoring** on your book

Learn how to **market and leverage** your book

REC

Record audio of your book while at retreat using the **Ultimate 48 Hour Author System**

We do the **transcription** of your audio

You **review & clean up** your transcript

We **edit** your book and then process your comments

Approved?

NO

YES

We create internal **book layout** and cover and send you the final book for approval

809107

Publishing
We do the **publishing work**

We send your book for **printing**

Print on demand set up and upload

1 proof copy printed

Approved

300 copies of your book delivered to your doorstep

IngramSpark

amazon ◄ ─ ─ Amazon

Go to **www.writeabook.com.au** to find out if you qualify to join the retreat

Ultimate 48 Hour Author Retreats

Each year we run the retreat in February, May, August and November. Go to www.writeabook.com.au to find this year's dates.

Attendance of an Ultimate 48 Hour Author Retreat is only permitted upon successful qualification. Not everyone who wants to write a book is a good match for our retreat. We do not work with fiction or children's books.

Ideally, you should first attend one of our Signature workshops called: Ultimate Blueprint for Book Writing Success.

We run these in all major cities around Australia 2-4 times per year depending on the size of the city. Melbourne is our home city and is where all the retreats are based — usually within an hour of Melbourne Airport at a beautiful retreat venue, starting midday on the Friday and finishing around 3pm on the Sunday. The majority of our authors (90%) are not locals to Melbourne and people from the US and New Zealand have travelled to attend one.

Find out when our next Ultimate Blueprint for Book Writing Success workshop is by going to the Workshops tab on writeabook.com.au

If you cannot make it to one of our Live events here is a link to a FREE Training you will love:
www.ultimate48hourauthor.com.au/webinar

NOTES

NOTES

NOTES

NOTES

NOTES

NOTES

NOTES

NOTES

NOTES

NOTES

NOTES

NOTES

NOTES

NOTES

NOTES

NOTES

NOTES

NOTES

NOTES

NOTES

NOTES

NOTES

NOTES

NOTES

NOTES

NOTES

NOTES

NOTES

NOTES

NOTES

www.ingramcontent.com/pod-product-compliance
Lightning Source LLC
Chambersburg PA
CBHW031854200326
41597CB00012B/400